Bible Baseball

Bible Baseball

840 Bible Questions and Answers
Graded into Singles, Doubles, Triples, Home Runs,
Sacrifices, and Bunts

by
ROBERT T. TAYLOR

MOODY PRESS
CHICAGO

9 10 11 12 Printing/LC/Year 95 94 93 92 91

ISBN 0-8024-0211-9

CONTENTS

Questions and Answers

INTRODUCTION

The game of Bible Baseball is familiar to thousands of people. Perhaps no one has done more to publicize this game than Dr. Robert T. Taylor, for eight years secretary of the Chicago Bible Society, who introduced new ideas into a game that had come to follow—in many cases—an almost stereotyped pattern of Bible questions and answers.

The innovations brought to the game by Dr. Taylor added life and enthusiasm and made the participants feel that they were playing a game of baseball, as well as answering questions on the Bible.

First of all, he graded the questions according to their degree of difficulty, into singles, doubles, triples, sacrifice, bunt, and home run groups. "The pitcher"—the one who puts the questions to the opposing team—therefore is required to use much skill in sizing up "the batter"—the one who is to answer the questions for the opposition.

Second, in order to develop into "championship form," the players on both teams need to go through a period of "spring training"—in this case, a study of the Scriptures on which questions for a given game will be based. If the questions are to be from the book of John, the "spring training camp" centers on that book. In this way, general study of the Scriptures and actual memorizing of certain key verses becomes an accomplished fact as a preliminary to the game itself.

Third, Dr. Taylor avoided use of all meaningless and trick questions. So far as possible, he tried to form questions that would bring out spiritual meaning and cultivate Bible understanding.

Let's see how a game of Bible Baseball actually works.

It is the sixth inning and the Westminster Church team and the Sixth Church team are tied 2 to 2. Westminster is at bat, one is out, and there are runners on first and third.

Joe Roberts is on third by virtue of answering a question good for a double. Ruth Ness went out on a question which, if answered correctly, would have been a triple. Then the Sixth Church pitcher tried a question good for a single: "Was Elisha a city, a prophet, or a mountain?" Usually light-hitting Isabel Scott answered correctly.

Now Paul Thomas is up and he can hit! The Sixth Church pitcher can try throwing a single—but it will mean a run if Paul hits. He decides to use a home run question, and his eye goes down the list for the very hardest one. He says clearly, "This is good for a home run—name four of Joseph's brothers." Paul thinks for ten seconds and then starts, "Benjamin, Reuben, Simeon, and, and, and—" (The timekeeper watches the second hand on his watch, for no answer can be delayed over thirty seconds). The time bell strikes and the umpire says, "Batter out," and looking at his answers adds, "Two others are Judah and Levi."

There are two out, and the next hitter proves to be an easy out on a question good for a triple. The Sixth Church pitcher has thrown a few of his hard questions, however, and—sure enough—Westminster puts over the winning run in the seventh on four successive singles. The box score reads,

Westminster—6 hits, 3 runs, 1 error.

Sixth Church—7 hits, 2 runs, no errors.

Westminster's error came when Susan Pratt blurted out an answer while her boyfriend was at bat, and he was automatically out.

The Chicago Bible Society is committed to the great task of the widest possible distribution and use of the Scriptures. We believe that Bible Baseball will prove an effective means of enlisting young people—and their elders as well—in Bible study and genuine enjoyment from participating in this wholesome game.

OFFICE OF EXECUTIVE SECRETARY
CHICAGO BIBLE SOCIETY
CHICAGO, ILLINOIS

RULES FOR BIBLE BASEBALL

1. The game is played with any number on each team.
2. A regular baseball diamond is laid out. The batter stands at the home plate, and the pitcher stands in the pitcher's box. Either chairs or pieces of newspaper laid on the floor can serve as bases.
3. Three books containing the Bible questions are needed for the game—one for each pitcher and the umpire. The umpire uses any means desired to decide which teams shall ask the "Red" and which the "Blue" questions.
4. There is a regular batting order, and the batters come to the plate in rotation.
5. The pitcher selects a question and says clearly, "The question is good for a single [double, triple, home run, as the case may be], and then he reads the question. If the batter fails to answer or answers incorrectly, the pitcher then reads the correct answer, and of course he will not want to use this question again unless he feels the opposing team is not paying attention to his reading of the answers.
6. If the batter answers the question correctly he moves to the place to which he is entitled. If he fails to answer he is out.
7. There are no balls and strikes in Bible Baseball. (By use of a sufficient number of questions the batter can be entitled to three strikes before he is called out, if this feature is agreed on, but this usually slows the game down too much.)
8. The pitcher will not repeat the question, and if the batter does not answer within thirty seconds of the conclusion of the statement of the question he is out.
9. Runners on base move forward in accordance with the number of bases for which the batter hits. That means that a runner on first base moves to third base if the batter hits a double. There is no such thing in Bible Baseball as a "fast man" being able to score from first on a double.
10. The rest of the game moves according to the rules of baseball.
11. There is an adult umpire, and the scorekeepers can be designated. The decisions of the umpire are absolutely final. If a batter is coached by a member of his own team he is automatically out, and his team is charged with an error. If he is "rattled" by the opposing team, that team is charged with an error and he takes his base.
12. Either the umpire or some other impartial person shall act as timekeeper.

MY EXPERIENCE
with
BIBLE BASEBALL

My association with Bible Baseball extends over a period of several years. My Junior and Intermediate Christian Endeavor in Tarrytown, New York, played the game consistently. We had teams in sectional leagues and in the Westchester County League and won a number of championships. We occasionally played Bible Baseball in adult groups and found it fun—although sometimes embarrassing.

We co-ordinated our Bible study with our Bible Baseball. Questions would be based on the book of the Bible being studied by the group. We included the quoting of Bible verses in the questions. Or discussion periods related life situations to our Scripture study.

Feeling often ran high in the games, but the advisor of the group always acted as umpire. There were many occasions where it became possible to apply biblical teachings to life situations that arose during the game. For example, a boy of twelve might be very agitated over a decision but would grin and see the inconsistency of his anger when the question thrown to him would be, "What did Jesus say should be done if a man compels you to go with him for one mile?"

We did not stop with Bible Baseball as a question and answer game. We used it to promote study and memorizing of the Scriptures. Every one of the thirty-five members of our Intermediate Christian Endeavor came into the church on confession of faith, and in a number of cases their parents joined the church at the same time. Every member of the society could conduct a worship service, which included leading in prayer. An effective means for teaching the Scriptures helped us in this training of our young people.

ROBERT T. TAYLOR

SET 1 — TEAM "RED"
1-Base Questions

1. What did Jesus say a man must do to see the kingdom of God? — Be born again. — John 3:7
2. Did Nicodemus refuse to believe earthly or heavenly things? — Earthly. — John 3:12
3. Who lifted up the serpent in the wilderness? — Moses. — John 3:14
4. Why did men love darkness better than light? — Because their deeds were evil. — John 3:19
5. What was the name of the well at which Jesus talked to the woman of Samaria? — Jacob's. — John 4:6
6. How did Jesus happen to be alone at a well in Samaria? — His disciples had gone to buy food. — John 4:8
7. Did Jesus approve of the personal life of the Samaritan woman? — No. — John 4:18
8. Did the Samaritan woman keep the interview with Jesus to herself? — No. — John 4:29
9. What two types of farm work did Jesus describe when He told of the fields that were ready to be harvested? — Sowing and reaping. — John 4:36
10. What did Jesus say about a prophet in his own country? — He said, "A prophet hath no honor in his own country." — John 4:44
11. In what city, often visited by Jesus, did the nobleman live whose son was healed by Jesus? — Capernaum. — John 4:46
12. When and how were people supposed to be cured at the Pool of Bethesda? — When the water was troubled, the first man in was healed. — John 5:4
13. What question did Jesus ask the man at the Pool of Bethesda which, to the man, seemed almost unnecessary? — Do you want to be cured: "Wilt thou be made whole?" — John 5:6
14. Who was described as "an Israelite, indeed, in which is no guile"? — Nathanael. — John 1:47
15. What did Jesus say to the lame man at the Pool of Bethesda? — "Rise, take up thy bed and walk." — John 5:8
16. What serious objection did the Jews have to the miracles of healing the man at the Pool of Bethesda and restoring the sight of the blind man? — They were performed on the Sabbath day. — John 9:14
17. What did Jesus say men should do about the Scriptures? — Search the Scriptures. — John 5:39
18. Why did Jesus ask Philip where bread was to be secured to feed the multitude? — To test Philip. — John 6:6
19. Whose will did Jesus seek to do? — The will of the Father. — John 6:38
20. Supply the missing word: "In the beginning was the _____." — "Word." — John 1:1
21. Who bore witness to the light? — John. — John 1:8
22. There was a man sent from God whose name was _____. — John. — John 1:6

13

23. To whom did John refer when he said, "Behold, the Lamb of God which taketh away the sin of the world"? — Jesus. — John 1:29
24. What does "Cephas" mean? — A stone. — John 1:42
25. In what city did Jesus attend a wedding? — In Cana of Galilee. — John 2:1
26. After Jesus fed the 5,000, what did the people want to do with Him? — Make Him a king. — John 6:15
27. What spiritual lesson did Jesus teach the people from the feeding of the multitude? — He said, "I am the bread of life." — John 6:35
28. When Jesus said to His twelve disciples, "Will ye also go away?" who answered Him? — Simon Peter answered, "Lord, to whom shall we go? Thou hast the words of eternal life. And we believe and are sure that thou art that Christ, the Son of the living God." — John 6:69
29. Why would Jesus not walk in Jewry? — The Jews sought to kill Him. — John 7:1
30. Did the brothers of Jesus believe in Him? — No. — John 7:5

2-Base Questions

1. Repeat John 3:16. — John 3:16
2. Were the Jews and the Samaritans reasonably friendly? — No. — John 4:9
3. Was the well at which Jesus talked with the woman of Samaria shallow or deep? — Deep. — John 4:11
4. When the Pharisees wanted to have Jesus killed, who suggested that it would be a good idea to hear His side of the story? — Nicodemus. — John 7:50
5. What reason did Jesus give for not going up to the Feast of Tabernacles as described in the seventh chapter of John? — He said, "My time is not yet come." — John 7:6
6. Near what market was the Pool of Bethesda? — The sheep market. — John 5:2
7. Did Jesus ever talk again with the man whom He healed at the Pool of Bethesda? — Yes, He said to him, "Sin no more, lest a worse thing come unto thee." — John 5:14
8. Who reported, "There is a lad here with food"? — Andrew, Simon Peter's brother. — John 6:9
9. An artist once painted a picture of the multitude sitting on rocks to be fed. What was wrong with that picture? — The people sat on the grass. — John 6:10
10. How many baskets of fragments of food were gathered up after the feeding of the multitude? — Twelve baskets. — John 6:13

3-Base Questions

1. Why did John baptize at Aenon, near Salim? — Because there was plenty of water there. — John 3:23
2. What did the disciples ask Jesus about the Samaritan woman? — Nothing. — John 4:27

14

3. How many porches did the Pool of Bethesda have?	Five porches.	John 5:2
4. What prophet did John quote?	Esaias.	John 1:23
5. Who remembered that it was written, "The zeal of thine house hath eaten me up"?	The disciples of Jesus.	John 2:17

Home-Run Questions

1. In what city in Samaria did Jesus talk with a woman at a well?	Sychar.	John 4:5
2. What attitude of mind is recorded in both the 3d and 4th chapters of John?	Marveling.	John 3:7 John 4:27
3. What length of time had one man been waiting at the pool of Bethesda?	38 years.	John 5:5
4. Why did the Jews first seek to kill Jesus?	Because He healed on the Sabbath. John 5:16	
5. The Jews sent priests and Levites from Jerusalem to ask what question?	"Who art thou?"	John 1:19
6. What bird is mentioned in each of the first two chapters of the gospel according to John?	The dove.	John 1:32 John 2:16
7. Name three men mentioned in the book of John who came from the same city.	Peter, Andrew, and Philip.	John 1:44
8. At the wedding at which Jesus turned the water into wine what was the capacity of the waterpots?	2 or 3 firkins apiece.	John 2:6
9. What three things did Jesus find being sold in the Temple at Jerusalem?	Oxen, sheep, doves.	John 2:14
10. To whom did Jesus say, "Make not my Father's house a house of merchandise"?	To those that sold doves.	John 2:16

Sacrifice-Fly Questions

(If answered correctly, the runners advance. Batter is out. Cannot be used with two out. Same rule applies to bunts.)

1. How many people does John tell us were fed from the food which the lad had?	Five thousand.	John 6:10
2. What does the word "Rabbi" mean?	Master.	John 1:38
3. Where did Jesus sit when He talked with the Samaritan woman?	By a well.	John 4:6

Bunt Questions

(Same rule as sacrifice.)

1. Is it true that men, in the time of Jesus, never let the women do such heavy work as carrying water?	No.	John 4:7
2. Did Jesus ever heal anyone without being with the person while He healed him?	Yes.	John 4:51

15

SET 1 – TEAM "BLUE"

1-Base Questions

1.	Who came to Jesus by night?	Nicodemus.	John 3:1
2.	What did Jesus say to Nicodemus that made him marvel?	That a man can be born again.	John 3:7
3.	Who was called by Jesus "a master in Israel"?	Nicodemus.	John 3:10
4.	Was it customary, in Galilee, to use the best or the poorest wine first?	The best was used first.	John 2:10
5.	When John's disciples told him that more people were going to Jesus than to him, was he jealous?	No.	John 3:28
6.	Did Nicodemus believe all that Jesus told him?	No.	John 3:12
7.	How did people, in the time of Jesus, get water out of wells?	They drew it up.	John 4:7
8.	What kind of water did Jesus offer the Samaritan woman?	A living water.	John 4:10
9.	How will the true worshipers worship the Father?	In spirit and in truth.	John 4:24
10.	Did the Samaritan woman get the water for which she went to the well?	No.	John 4:28
11.	Why did the Samaritan woman think Jesus might be the Christ?	Because He told her all the things she ever did.	John 4:29
12.	Did any of the Samaritans from the city of the woman at the well believe on Jesus?	Yes.	John 4:39
13.	What kind of people gathered around the pool of Bethesda?	Afflicted people.	John 5:3
14.	What difficulty did the man of the Pool of Bethesda have in getting into the Pool?	He did not have anyone to put him into the Pool, so someone else always got there first.	John 5:7
15.	Give another name for the Sea of Tiberias.	The Sea of Galilee.	John 6:1
16.	Will Jesus receive anyone who comes to Him, believing?	Yes: "Him that cometh to me, I will in no wise cast out."	John 6:37
17.	Did Jesus know, in the early days of His ministry, that one of His own disciples would betray Him?	Yes.	John 6:64
18.	What did the Pharisees say about the possibility of a prophet's coming out of Galilee?	They said that a prophet couldn't come out of Galilee.	John 8:41
19.	What was the light of men?	Life.	John 1:4
20.	Who gave the law?	Moses.	John 1:17
21.	When two disciples asked Jesus where He lived, what did He say?	"Come and see."	John 1:39
22.	Who said, "Can there any good thing come out of Nazareth?"	Nathanael.	John 1:46
23.	What man did Jesus see sitting under a fig tree before the man even knew Jesus?	Nathanael.	John 1:48

24.	What was the first miracle performed by Jesus?	Turning water into wine. John 2:11
25.	Why was it that Jesus did not need for anyone to testify of man?	"He knew what was in man." John 2:25
26.	When Jesus refused to go with his brothers to the Feast of the Tabernacles in Jerusalem, did He go to the feast?	Yes, He went in secret to Jerusalem. John 7:10
27.	When the disciples crossed the Sea of Tiberias after the feeding of the multitude, how did Jesus get across the sea?	He walked part way on the water and joined the disciples in the ship. John 6:19
28.	Did some of the disciples of Jesus quit at any time and never come back to Him again?	Yes, there were some who started out to follow Him and didn't have the courage to keep on. John 6:66
29.	What did the Israelites eat in the wilderness?	Manna. John 6:31
30.	Did the brothers of Jesus want Him to go to Jerusalem for the Feast of the Tabernacles?	Yes. John 7:3

2-Base Questions

1.	Did Jesus baptize people?	No. John 4:2
2.	When the officers came to the chief priests and did not bring Jesus with them, what reason did they give?	They said, "Never man spake like this man." John 7:46
3.	When Jesus talked with the woman in Samaria, how long was it before harvest?	Four months. John 4:35
4.	Did Jesus ever return to the city in which He made water into wine?	Yes. John 4:46
5.	What was the second miracle that Jesus did in Galilee?	He healed the nobleman's son. John 4:54
6.	After Jesus healed the man at the Pool of Bethesda, did He stand around and talk to the people?	No. John 5:13
7.	What was the problem when a great multitude followed Jesus to a mountain to hear Him preach?	The people were hungry and there was no food. John 6:5
8.	As told in the sixth chapter of John, how much food did the boy have in his basket?	Five barley loaves and two small fishes. John 6:9
9.	What was there about the teachings of Jesus that made the Jews marvel?	He was educated without all of the formal schooling of the Jews. John 7:15
10.	When the multitude was fed, was there any fish left over?	No; they gathered up "fragments of the five barley loaves." John 6:13

3-Base Questions

1.	What happy event is mentioned in both the second and third chapters of John?	A wedding. John 2:1 John 3:29
2.	Did the Woman of Samaria have any idea that Christ was coming?	Yes. John 4:25

3. What color were the fields in Palestine when the grain was ready to be harvested? — White. — John 4:35

4. Did more people believe in Jesus because of His own word or because of what the woman at the well told them? — Because of His own word. — John 4:41

5. Was Elias one of those who followed Jesus? — No. — John 1:21

Home-Run Questions

1. To what element did Jesus liken the Spirit? — The wind. — John 3:8

2. At what time of day did Jesus rest by the well in Samaria? — The sixth hour. — John 4:6

3. When Jesus talked with the woman at the well, why was He in Samaria? — He had to go through Samaria to get from Judea to Galilee. — John 4:4

4. How long did Jesus stay with the Samaritans of the city of the woman at the well? — Two days. — John 4:40

5. What did Jesus say that infuriated the Jews even more than the first reason and made them want to kill Him? — He taught the truth that God was His Father. — John 10:31

6. Where did John first baptize? — In Bethabara, beyond Jordan. — John 1:28

7. Who was Simon Peter's brother? — Andrew. — John 1:40

8. How many waterpots were there at the wedding where Jesus turned the water into wine? — Six. — John 2:6

9. What did Jesus drive out of the Temple with the scourge of small cords? — The money changers; the sheep; the oxen. (If doves are included the answer is wrong). — John 2:15

10. How long did it take to build the Temple in Jerusalem? — Forty-six years. — John 2:20

Sacrifice-Fly Questions

(If answered correctly, the runners advance. Batter is out. Cannot be used with two out. Same rule applies to bunts.)

1. Did everyone in the multitude that Jesus fed have enough to eat? — Yes. — John 6:11

2. Were the Pharisees Jews or Gentiles? — Jews. — John 3:1

3. Did Jesus ever attend a social event? — Yes, a wedding. — John 2:2

Bunt Questions

(Same rule as sacrifice.)

1. Did the people of Galilee ever go to Jerusalem? — Yes. — John 4:45

2. Who betrayed Jesus? — Judas Iscariot. — John 6:71

SET 2 — TEAM "RED"

1-Base Questions

1. Who visited the Mount of Olives? — Jesus. John 8:1
2. What did Jesus tell the woman taken in adultery to do? — "Go, and sin no more." John 8:11
3. In the 8th chapter of John, where did Jesus stand when He taught in the Temple? — "In the treasury." John 8:20
4. Why did Jesus say the Jews were in bondage? — Because they were the servants of sin. John 8:34
5. Why did Jesus say the Jews did not acknowledge God as their Father? — Because they rejected Jesus. John 8:42
6. Who is the father of lying? — The devil. John 8:44
7. What did Jesus do with clay? — Put it on the blind man's eyes. John 9:6
8. To whom did they take the man who had been blind? — To the Pharisees. John 9:13
9. What punishment did the Jews decree for anyone who confessed Jesus as Christ? — To be put out of the synagogue. John 9:22
10. Who climbs into the sheepfold? — The thief. John 10:1
11. Who opens the door of the sheepfold? — The porter. John 10:3
12. When the shepherd takes out his sheep where does he walk? — Ahead of them. John 10:4
13. Why do the sheep flee from a stranger? — They do not know his voice. John 10:5
14. Finish this sentence: "I am come that they might have life _____." — "and that they might have it more abundantly." John 10:10
15. What does the hireling do when trouble comes? — He runs. John 10:12
16. Who doesn't care anything about the sheep? — The hireling. John 10:13
17. Does Jesus have any other sheep? — Yes. John 10:16
18. Where was Solomon's porch? — In the Temple. John 10:23
19. Who anointed Jesus with ointment and wiped His feet with her hair? — Mary, the sister of Lazarus. John 11:2
20. When Jesus said, "Lazarus sleepeth," what did He mean? — He knew Lazarus was dead. John 11:13
21. How long had Lazarus been dead when Jesus came to his grave? — Four days. John 11:17
22. Finish this great statement by Jesus: "I am the resurrection _____." — "and the life: he that believeth in me, though he were dead, yet shall he live." John 11:25
23. Who betrayed Jesus? — Judas Iscariot. John 12:4
24. How was Jesus greeted when He came to Jerusalem for the feast of the Passover? — With palm branches and praise. John 12:13
25. Men of what nationality came seeking Jesus in Jerusalem? — Greeks. John 12:20
26. Finish this sentence: "Father, save me from this hour: but for _____." — "this cause came I unto this hour." John 12:27
27. How did Jesus signify who would betray Him? — By giving him a sop. John 13:26

28. Who kept the money bag for the disciples? | Judas. | John 12:6

29. How many times was a disciple going to deny Jesus before the crowing of the cock? | Three times. | John 13:38

30. Fill in the missing words:
1—"In my Father's house are _____." | "many mansions: if it were not so, I would have told you. I go to prepare a place for you.

2—"_____ there ye may be also." | "And if I go and prepare a place for you, I will come again, and receive you unto myself; that where I am . . ." John 14:3

2-Base Questions

1. In Jewish law the testimony of how many men was true? | Two men. | John 8:17

2. Finish this verse: "And ye shall know the truth, _____." | "and the truth shall make you free." John 8:32

3. By what method did the Jews often seek to kill Jesus? | Stoning. | John 10:31

4. Finish this verse: "He answered and said, "Whether he be a sinner or no, I know not: one thing I know _____." | "that, whereas I was blind, now I see." John 9:25

5. What was the name of the high priest who counseled that Jesus should be put to death? | Caiaphas. | John 11:49

6. How much did the ointment used by Mary weigh? | One pound. | John 12:3

7. Who beckoned to the disciple whom Jesus loved to get him to ask Jesus a question? | Simon Peter. | John 13:24

8. Who said to Jesus, "Lord, we know not whither thou goest"? | Thomas. | John 14:5

9. How does John distinguish one Judas from the other? | By the words *not Iscariot*. | John 14:22

10. Finish this sentence: "Peace I leave with you, my peace I give unto you: not as _____." | "the world giveth, give I unto you. Let not your heart be troubled, neither let it be afraid." John 14:27

3-Base Questions

1. What reason did the Pharisees give for saying the record that Jesus bore was not true? | They accused Him of bearing record of Himself. | John 8:13

2. Who, when he thought Jesus was going to certain death, made the courageous statement "Let us also go, that we may die with Him"? | Thomas. | John 11:16

3. Who told Jesus of the men who came saying, "Sir, we would see Jesus"? | Andrew and Philip. | John 12:22

4. How will men know we are the disciples of Jesus? | If we love one another. | John 13:35

5. Who said, "Lord, show us the Father and it sufficeth us"? | Philip. | John 14:8

20

Home-Run Questions

1. Who came first, Jesus or Abraham? — Jesus. — John 8:58
2. Give another meaning for "Siloam." — Sent. — John 9:7
3. For what three reasons does a thief come to the sheepfold? — (1) To steal; (2) to kill; (3) to destroy. — John 10:10
4. Where did Jesus go when He left Judea? — To Bethabara. — John 1:28
5. When Jesus came near the home of Lazarus what did the two sisters do that was entirely typical of their characters? — Martha came to meet Him, but Mary sat still in the house. — John 11:20
6. Where did Mary and Martha meet Jesus at the time of the death of Lazarus? — Outside the town. — John 11:30
7. What illustration of planting, from the processes of nature, did Jesus use in regard to His death? — The grain must die before it grows. — John 12:24
8. What was the new commandment that Jesus gave His disciples? — "That ye love one another; as I have loved you, that ye also love one another." — John 13:34
9. What did Jesus say men should do if they loved Him? — Keep His commandments. — John 14:15
10. Which chapter of the first 14 of John has the most verses? — Chapter 6 (71 verses).

Sacrifice-Fly Questions

(If answered correctly, the runners advance. Batter is out. Cannot be used with two out. Same rule applies to bunts.)

1. Why did the blind man believe that Jesus must be from God? — Because He healed him. — John 9:33
2. Who was told that he would deny Jesus? — Peter. — John 13:38
3. Did Martha know Jesus to be the Christ? — Yes. — John 11:27

Bunt Questions

(Same rule as sacrifice.)

1. How did the blind man make a living? — He begged. — John 9:8
2. Did the blind man believe on Jesus? — Yes. — John 9:38

SET 2—TEAM "BLUE"

1-Base Questions

1. Who did Jesus say should cast the first stone at the woman taken in adultery? — "He that is without sin." — John 8:7
2. Who judged after the flesh? — The Pharisees. — John 8:15
3. When are men free indeed? — If Jesus makes them free. — John 8:36
4. In whom is there no truth? — The devil. — John 8:44
5. Why did the parents of the blind man refuse to give any information? — Because they feared the Jews. — John 9:22
6. Who comes into the sheepfold by the door? — The shepherd. — John 10:2
7. How does the shepherd call his own sheep? — By name. — John 10:3
8. Why do the sheep follow the shepherd? — They know his voice. — John 10:4
9. Who is the door for the sheepfold? — Jesus. — John 10:7
10. How much will the good shepherd do for his sheep? — Give his life. — John 10:11
11. What animal catches the sheep? — The wolf. — John 10:12
12. Finish this verse: "As the Father knoweth me, even so know I the Father: and I _____." — "lay down my life for the sheep." — John 10:15
13. What season was it at the Feast of the Dedication? — Winter. — John 10:22
14. Why did the Jews say they wanted to kill Jesus? — For blasphemy. — John 10:33
15. Why did the disciples of Jesus not want Him to go back to Judea? — Because the Jews were trying to kill Him. — John 11:8
16. Give another name for Didymus. — Thomas. — John 11:16
17. Why did the Jews come to Mary and Martha? — To comfort them. — John 11:19
18. What did Jesus do before the grave of Lazarus? — He wept and prayed. — John 11:35 John 11:41
19. Whom had the chief priests and the Pharisees commanded to help them catch Jesus? — Anyone who knew where He was. — John 11:57
20. How many days before the Passover did Jesus return to Bethany? — Six days. — John 12:1
21. Was Judas really interested in the poor? — No. — John 12:6
22. Finish this sentence: "Blessed is the King of _____." — "Israel that cometh in the name of the Lord." — John 12:13
23. Who said, "Sir, we would see Jesus"? — Certain Greeks. — John 12:21
24. Finish this sentence: "For they loved the praise of men _____." — "more than the praise of God." — John 12:43
25. Why did Jesus wash the feet of the disciples? — To give them an example. — John 13:15
26. Why did the disciples of Jesus think He had sent Judas out? — Either to buy something or to give something to the poor. — John 13:29
27. Who said he would lay down his life for Jesus? — Peter. — John 13:37

28. Finish this verse: "Let not your heart be troubled, ye believe _____." "in God, believe also in me." John 14:1
29. Who was the father of Judas Iscariot? Simon. John 13:26
30. Did any of the chief rulers believe in Jesus? Yes. John 12:42

2-Base Questions

1. Finish this verse: "Then said Jesus to those Jews which believed on him, If ye continue in My word _____." "then are ye my disciples indeed." John 8:31
2. Whose descendants did the Pharisees claim to be? Abraham's. John 8:33
3. What did the Jews do that Abraham had not done? Seek to destroy one who brought truth from God. John 8:40
4. What kind of ointment did Mary use in anointing the feet of Jesus? Spikenard. John 12:3
5. Why did the chief priests want to put Lazarus to death? Because he caused the people to believe in Jesus. John 12:11
6. Who questioned Jesus when He washed the feet of the disciples? Peter. John 13:6
7. After He signified that Judas would betray Him, what did Jesus say to him? "That thou doest, do quickly." John 13:27
8. Give two other names for the Comforter. Spirit of Truth. John 14:17
The Holy Ghost. John 14:26
9. Finish this sentence: "Let not your heart be troubled _____." "neither let it be afraid." John 14:27
10. Why did Jesus tell His disciples about His crucifixion before it came to pass? So they would believe when it did come to pass. John 14:29

3-Base Questions

1. In what pool did Jesus tell the blind man to wash? Siloam. John 9:7
2. Name three members of a family that lived in Bethany. Lazarus, Mary, Martha. John 11:1
3. When did Jesus say a man stumbles? When he walks in the night. John 11:10
4. To whom were these words addressed: "Sir, we would see Jesus"? To Philip. John 12:21
5. The saying of what prophet was fulfilled in the lack of belief in Jesus? Esaias. John 12:38

Home-Run Questions

1. How many times did the blind man describe the way in which Jesus healed him? Twice. John 9:11
John 9:15
2. Who really took the life of Jesus from Him? No man. He laid it down of Himself. John 10:18
3. How far was Bethany from Jerusalem? Fifteen furlongs. John 11:18
4. Was it Mary or Martha who said to Jesus, "Lord, if thou hadst been here, my brother had not died"? Both of them. John 11:21
John 11:32

5. To what city did Jesus go after He had been in Bethany?	Ephraim.	John 11:54
6. What was the value, in money, of the ointment used by Mary?	Three hundred pence.	John 12:5
7. Who was leaning on the breast of Jesus at the Last Supper?	John. (He does not use his own name because he is the writer of this gospel.) John 13:23	
8. What did Jesus answer the disciple who said, "How can we know the way?"	"I am the way, the truth, and the life." John 14:6	
9. What are the last five words of the 14th chapter of John?	"Arise, let us go hence."	John 14:31
10. Which chapter in the first fourteen of John has the least number of verses?	Chapter 2 (25 verses).	

Sacrifice-Fly Questions

(If answered correctly, the runners advance. Batter is out. Cannot be used with two out. Same rule applies to bunts.)

1. Who is the Good Shepherd?	Jesus.	John 10:11
2. Who said, "The poor always ye have with you"?	Jesus.	John 12:8
3. Whom did Jesus raise from the dead?	Lazarus.	John 11:44

Bunt Questions

(Same rule as sacrifice.)

1. On what day did Jesus heal the blind man?	On the Sabbath.	John 9:14
2. What relation was Martha to Lazarus?	She was his sister.	John 11:3

SET 3 — TEAM "RED"

1-Base Questions

1. Finish this statement: "I am the vine, _____." | "Ye are the branches." | John 15:5
2. Who is the greater, the servant or his lord? | His lord. | John 15:20
3. Complete this statement: "But be of good cheer; _____." | "I have overcome the world." | John 16:33
4. Did Jesus pray only for His disciples? | No. | John 17:20
5. Where did Jesus often go with His disciples? | To a garden. | John 18:2
6. Which disciple was known to the high priest? | John. | John 18:16
7. How many disciples went into the palace of the high priest? | Two. | John 18:16
8. Complete this statement: "Thy word is _____." | "Truth." | John 17:17
9. What proof did Jesus offer Pilate that His kingdom is not of this world? | His servants did not fight. | John 18:36
10. Did Pilate find any fault in Jesus? | No. | John 18:38
11. Who said: "Behold the man!" | Pilate. | John 19:5
12. Did Pilate want to release Jesus? | Yes. | John 19:12
13. Complete this statement: "The chief priests answered, 'We have no king _____.' " | "but Caesar." | John 19:15
14. Complete this statement: "What I have written _____." | "I have written." | John 19:22
15. How did the soldiers decide who should have the coat of Jesus? | By casting lots. | John 19:24
16. Who was a secret disciple? | Joseph of Arimathea. | John 19:38
17. On what day of the week did Mary come to the sepulchre? | The first. | John 20:1
18. What two disciples did Mary tell about the empty tomb? | Peter and John. | John 20:2
19. What did Mary see when she looked in the sepulchre? | Two angels. | John 20:12
20. Who did Mary think the risen Lord was at first? | The gardener. | John 20:15
21. When did Mary recognize Jesus in the garden? | When He called her by name. | John 20:16
22. What did Jesus say first when He appeared to His disciples after He had risen? | "Peace be unto you." | John 20:19
23. On what day of the week did the risen Lord first appear to His disciples? | The first. | John 20:19
24. Does John record all Jesus did after He rose from the dead? | No. | John 20:30
25. Which disciple proposed going fishing? | Peter. | John 21:3
26. Which disciple was from Cana? | Nathanael. | John 21:2
27. What did Peter do out in the boat when he knew Jesus was on shore? | Jumped into the sea. | John 21:7

28.	Which disciple was curious about what would happen to another disciple?	Peter.	John 21:21
29.	How many chapters are in the gospel of John?	Twenty-one.	
30.	Did the disciples pull their large catch of fish into the ship?	No.	John 21:11

2-Base Questions

1.	Finish this verse: "This is my commandment, That ye love _____."	"one another, as I have loved you." John 15:12	
2.	Complete this verse: "I have yet many things to say unto you, but _____."	"ye cannot bear them now." John 16:12	
3.	Who said that it was expedient that one man should die for the people?	Caiaphas.	John 18:14
4.	What was the name of the man to whom Jesus was led away from the garden?	Annas.	John 18:13
5.	Who first struck Jesus?	An officer of the high priest.	John 18:22
6.	Where was Jesus taken from the palace of the high priest?	To the hall of judgment.	John 18:28
7.	Whom did the Jews want released instead of Jesus?	Barabbas.	John 18:40
8.	What did Jesus say first, the second time He appeared to His disciples?	"Peace be unto you."	John 20:26
9.	Were the doors open or shut when Jesus appeared to His disciples?	Shut.	John 20:19
10.	Did the disciples expect Jesus to rise from the dead?	No.	John 20:9

3-Base Questions

1.	What disciple was from the city where Jesus performed His first miracle?	Nathanael.	John 21:2
2.	What did Jesus say that grieved Peter?	He asked Peter the third time, "Lovest thou Me?" John 21:17	
3.	What did Pilate write on the cross?	"Jesus of Nazareth, the King of the Jews." John 19:19	
4.	What did the objectors want to add to what was written on the cross?	"He said."	John 19:21
5.	Into whose care did Jesus deliver His mother?	John.	John 19:26

Home-Run Questions

1.	Whose ear was cut off?	Malchus's.	John 18:10
2.	How many times did Jesus say to Peter, "Lovest thou me?"	Three times.	John 21:17
3.	How many fish were in the net described in John 21?	One hundred fifty-three.	John 21:11
4.	What mention is made of a relative of the man whose ear was cut off?	He tells Peter he saw him with Jesus. John 18:26	
5.	At what hour did Pilate deliver Jesus to be crucified?	About the sixth hour.	John 19:14

6. Give the Hebrew name for the place of the skull.   Golgotha.   John 19:17

7. Name two men who engaged in a famous foot race.   John and Peter.   John 20:4

8. What specific commission did Jesus give Peter?   "Feed my sheep."   John 21:17

9. What was used for light by those who came to take Jesus in the garden?   Lanterns and torches.   John 18:3

10. Complete this verse: "Thomas, because thou hast seen me, thou hast believed: _____."   "Blessed are they that have not seen, and yet have believed."   John 20:29

Sacrifice-Fly Questions

(If answered correctly, the runners advance. Batter is out. Cannot be used with two out. Same rule applies to bunts.)

1. What is the greatest sign of love?   To give your life for a friend.   John 15:13

2. Did Jesus want His disciples to fight?   No.   John 18:11

3. What was the name of the Roman before whom Jesus was tried?   Pilate.   John 19:12

Bunt Questions

(Same rule as sacrifice.)

1. Were the Pharisees for or against Jesus?   Against.   John 18:3

2. What signal came after a disciple denied Jesus?   The cock crew.   John 18:27

SET 3—TEAM "BLUE"

1-Base Questions

1. In whom were the disciples to abide? — Jesus. — John 15:4
2. Finish this statement: "For without me ye _____." — "can do nothing." — John 15:5
3. If a man hates Jesus does he also hate the Father? — Yes. — John 15:23
4. Did Jesus pray that His disciples should be taken out of the world? — No. — John 17:15
5. With whom did Judas stand in the garden? — Those who were coming to take Jesus. — John 18:5
6. Which one of the disciples had a sword? — Peter. — John 18:10
7. Was there a man or a woman doorkeeper at the palace of the high priest? — A woman. — John 18:16
8. To what person did Peter deny Jesus the first time? — The doorkeeper of the palace. — John 18:17
9. What happened after the last time Peter denied Jesus? — The cock crew. — John 18:27
10. What did Pilate ask about truth? — "What is truth?" — John 18:38
11. What kind of crown did the soldiers place on the head of Jesus? — Thorns. — John 19:2
12. What ruler did Pilate serve? — Caesar. — John 19:12
13. What political pressure did the Jews bring on Pilate? — They said he would not be Caesar's friend if he let Jesus go. — John 19:12
14. Was Jesus crucified alone? — No. — John 19:18
15. How many parts did the soldiers make of the clothes of Jesus? — Four. — John 19:23
16. Where did the mother of Jesus live after the crucifixion? — In John's home — John 19:27
17. Who was Nicodemus? — The man who came to Jesus by night. — John 19:39
18. Which Mary came to the sepulchre? — Mary Magdalene. — John 20:1
19. Who lingered at the empty tomb? — Mary. — John 20:11
20. What was Mary doing when she looked in the sepulchre? — Weeping. — John 20:13
21. What did Jesus first say to Mary in the garden? — "Woman, why weepest thou?" — John 20:15
22. What does Rabboni mean? — Master. — John 20:16
23. Which disciple doubted the resurrection of Jesus? — Thomas. — John 20:25
24. Complete this verse: "And Thomas answered and said unto him, 'My Lord _____.'" — "and my God." — John 20:28
25. How many days after the resurrection did Thomas see Jesus? — Eight. — John 20:26
26. Which disciple was called Didymus? — Thomas. — John 21:2
27. Did the disciples fish in the day or night? — Night. — John 21:3
28. What did Jesus give His disciples to eat at a famous breakfast? — Bread and fish. — John 21:13

29. How many books did John suppose could be written about the life of Christ? — More than the world could contain. John 21:25

30. Did the disciples go fishing in a large or a small ship? — Small. John 21:8

2-Base Questions

1. Finish this verse: "If ye abide in me, and my words abide in you _____." — "ye shall ask what ye will and it shall be done unto you." John 15:7

2. What did Jesus call his disciples instead of servants? — Friends. John 15:15

3. Complete this verse: "And this is life eternal _____." — "That they might know thee the only true God, and Jesus Christ, whom Thou hast sent." John 17:3

4. Which disciples followed Jesus when He was taken before the high priest? — Peter and John. John 18:15

5. How did Jesus say the high priest could learn all about His teaching? — Ask those who had heard Him teach. John 18:21

6. When Jesus was struck a blow, what did Peter do? — Stood by the fire denying Jesus. John 18:25

7. Why didn't the Jews want to judge Jesus according to their own law? — They were not allowed to impose the death penalty. John 18:31

8. Complete this statement: "Jesus answered, "Thou couldest have no power at all against me _____." — "except it were given thee from above." John 19:11

9. What did Jesus say first when He appeared to His disciples by the sea? — "Children, have ye any meat?" John 21:5

10. Were the disciples still afraid of the Jews after the death of Jesus? — Yes. John 20:19

3-Base Questions

1. By what sea did Jesus show Himself to His disciples? — Tiberias. John 21:1

2. Did the disciples know the risen Lord when He first appeared by the sea? — No. John 21:4

3. How many days was it between the first and second appearances of the risen Lord to His disciples? — Eight. John 20:26

4. Who objected to what was written on the cross? — The chief priests. John 19:21

5. What description is given of the coat of Jesus? — It had no seam. John 19:23

Home-Run Questions

1. In what chapter of the gospel of John is Jesus the only speaker? — Chapter 17. John 17

2. What relation was Annas to Caiaphas? — Father-in-law. John 18:13

3. What was Cedron? — A brook. John 18:1

4. Did the Jews take Jesus into the hall of judgment? — No. John 18:28

5. Give the Hebrew name for the place called the Pavement. — Gabbatha. John 19:13

6.	In what languages was the title on the cross written?	Hebrew, Greek, and Latin. John 19:20
7.	Give proof that Pilate knew several languages.	He wrote on the cross in three languages. John 19:19-20
8.	Complete this verse: "I am the true vine, and _____."	"My Father is the husbandman." John 15:1
9.	Did Jesus say that John would not die?	No. John 21:23
10.	Was the night of the Lord's trial warm or cold?	Cold. John 18:18

Sacrifice-Fly Questions

(If answered correctly, the runners advance. Batter is out. Cannot be used with two out. Same rule applies to bunts.)

1.	What is done with unfruitful branches?	They are burned. John 15:6
2.	In what did a man carry a sword?	A sheath. John 18:11
3.	Give another name for Simon.	Peter. John 18:15

Bunt Questions

(Same rule as sacrifice.)

1.	Who betrayed Jesus?	Judas. John 18:5
2.	Which disciple denied Jesus?	Peter. John 18:27

SET 4—TEAM "RED"

1-Base Questions

1. Who came preaching in the wilderness, clothed in camel's hair? — John the Baptist. — Mark 1:6

2. In what work were Simon and Andrew engaged when Jesus called them to follow Him? — Fishing. — Mark 1:16

3. Whose mother-in-law did Jesus heal? — Simon Peter's. — Mark 1:30-31

4. In what ingenious way did four men get a man sick of the palsy to Jesus? — They let him down through the roof. — Mark 2:4

5. What became of the seed that fell by the wayside? — The birds ate it. — Mark 4:4

6. What became of the seed that fell among thorns? — The thorns choked it. — Mark 4:7

7. To what kind of seed did Jesus liken the kingdom of God? — The mustard seed. — Mark 4:31

8. Jesus sent devils into a herd of what kind of animals? — Swine. — Mark 5:13

9. Finish this statement, "A prophet is not without honor. but _____." — "in his own country." — Mark 6:4

10. Jesus had compassion on the multitude because they were as sheep without what? — A shepherd. — Mark 6:34

11. After the feeding of the five thousand Jesus went alone to a mountain; what was His purpose? — To pray. — Mark 6:46

12. Jesus once fed five thousand. How many thousand did He feed at another time? — Four. — Mark 8:9

13. Did the man who "saw men as trees, walking" ever have any improvement in his vision? — Yes. — Mark 8:25

14. When Jesus predicted His suffering and death, which disciple rebuked Him? — Peter. — Mark 8:32

15. Finish this sentence: "For whosoever will save his life shall _____." — "lose it." — Mark 8:35

16. Did Jesus tell His disciples to forbid men to cast out devils in His name? — No. — Mark 9:39

17. A young man came to Jesus asking what he could do to inherit eternal life. What did Jesus tell him to do that sent him away grieved? — Sell all that he had and give to the poor. — Mark 10:21

18. When Jesus sent two disciples to bring a colt, did anyone question them? — Yes. — Mark 11:5

19. What did Jesus do to those who bought and sold in the Temple? — He cast them out. — Mark 11:15

20. If you had an old Roman penny from the time of Christ whose picture would be on it? — Caesar's. — Mark 12:16

21. Why did Jesus say that the widow who put two mites in the collection box had put in more than all the others? — Because she gave all she had. Mark 12:44

22. Did Jesus warn His disciples against false christs? — Yes. Mark 13:22

23. When Jesus sent two of His disciples to prepare the Passover, they were to follow what man? — A man carrying a pitcher of water. Mark 14:13

24. When Jesus told His disciples one of them would betray Him, what did they begin to ask Him? — "Is it I?" Mark 14:19

25. What one thing did Jesus do before He gave the cup to His disciples at the Last Supper? — He gave thanks. Mark 14:23

26. What did the disciples do while Jesus was praying in Gethsemane? — They went to sleep. Mark 14:37

27. What injury was suffered by a servant of the high priest? — His ear was cut off. Mark 14:47

28. Before what Roman ruler was Jesus tried? — Pilate. Mark 15:1

29. To whom did Jesus first appear after His resurrection? — Mary Magdalene. Mark 16:9

30. When the Pharisees and Herodians asked Jesus if they should pay taxes, He asked them to bring Him what? — A penny. Mark 12:15

2-Base Questions

1. Who ate locusts and wild honey? — John the Baptist. Mark 1:6

2. For how long was Jesus tempted by Satan in the wilderness? — Forty days. Mark 1:13

3. What kind of grain did Jesus and His disciples eat on Sunday? — Corn. Not Western "corn"; likely barley or wheat. Mark 2:23

4. Who put Salome up to the request that she made of the king? — Her mother, Herodias. Mark 6:24

5. Finish this sentence: "For what shall it profit a man, if he shall gain the whole world, and _____?" — "lose his own soul?" Mark 8:36

6. Finish this sentence: "This kind can come forth by nothing but by _____." — "prayer and fasting." Mark 9:29

7. Finish this statement: "It is easier for a camel to go through the eye of a needle, than _____." — "for a rich man to enter into the kingdom of God." Mark 10:25

8. Finish this statement: "Render to Caesar the things that are Caesar's and to _____." — "God, the things that are God's." Mark 12:17

9. Finish this statement: "And the second is like, namely this, thou shalt _____." — "love thy neighbor as thyself." Mark 12:31

10. Immediately after Jesus was anointed with the precious ointment, one of the disciples left the room. Which disciple was it? — Judas. Mark 14:10

32

3-Base Questions

1. Finish this verse: "And Jesus said unto them, Come ye after me, and I will make you to become fishers _____."
   "of men." Mark 1:17

2. Finish this verse: "And if a kingdom be divided against itself, that kingdom _____."
   "cannot stand." Mark 3:24

3. Finish this sentence: "Whosoever will come after me, let him deny himself, and take _____."
   "up his cross, and follow me." Mark 8:34

4. Supply the missing words: "For even the Son of Man came not _____, but to _____ and to give his life a ransom for many."
   "to be ministered unto,"
   "minister" Mark 10:45

5. In whose house was Jesus anointed from a box of precious ointment?
   Simon the leper's. Mark 14:3

Home-Run Questions

1. Was John the Baptist another name for John the son of Zebedee?
   No. Mark 1:19 Mark 6:24

2. Did Jesus say, "No man seweth a piece of old cloth on a new garment"?
   No, He said, "No man seweth a piece of new cloth on an old garment." Mark 2:21

3. Who ate the shew-bread?
   David. Mark 2:25

4. Who said his name was Legion?
   The man with the unclean spirit. Mark 5:9

5. When the five thousand to be fed sat down on the grass in ranks, how many were in each group?
   One hundred in some and fifty in others. Mark 6:40

6. When Jesus asked His disciples "Whom do men say that I am?" what three answers did the disciples give?
   John the Baptist. Mark 8:28
   Elias.
   One of the prophets.

7. How many chapters are there in the book of Mark?
   Sixteen.

8. With what two Old Testament figures did Jesus talk on the mount of transfiguration?
   Elias. Mark 9:4
   Moses.

9. What two brothers wanted to sit, one on the right hand and one on the left hand of Jesus?
   James and John. Mark 10:35

10. After Jesus rode into Jerusalem in triumph, where did He spend the night?
    In Bethany. Mark 11:11

Sacrifice-Fly Questions

(If answered correctly, the runners advance. Batter is out. Cannot be used with two out. Same rule applies to bunts.)

1. On what day did Jesus heal the man with the withered hand?
   The Sabbath. Mark 3:2, 5

2. Did Jesus approve of divorce?   No.   Mark 10:11-12
3. What was the affliction of Bartimaeus?   He was blind.   Mark 10:46

Bunt Questions

(Same rule as sacrifice.)

1. Which disciple betrayed Jesus?   Judas.   Mark 14:43
2. With what sign was Jesus betrayed?   A kiss.   Mark 14:45

SET 4 — TEAM "BLUE"
1-Base Questions

1. Of whom did John say, "There cometh one mightier than I after me, the latchet of whose shoes I am not worthy to stoop down and unloose"?

   Jesus.   Mark 1:7, 9

2. Who was the brother of John?

   James.   Mark 1:19

3. Who ministered to Jesus when He was in the wilderness with the wild beasts?

   The angels.   Mark 1:13

4. How many did Jesus ordain as disciples?

   Twelve.   Mark 3:14

5. What became of the seed that fell on stony ground?

   It withered.   Mark 4:6

6. Who said to a man, "Thou art not far from the kingdom of God"?

   Jesus.   Mark 12:34

7. What became of the seed that fell on good ground?

   It grew.   Mark 4:8

8. What did Jesus say to the wind and waves during a storm on the lake?

   "Peace, be still."   Mark 4:39

9. Did the people in the country of the Gadarenes beg Jesus to stay with them after He had cast the devils out of the man?

   No, they asked Him to leave.   Mark 5:17

10. What request did Salome make of the king?

    The head of John the Baptist on a charger.   Mark 6:25

11. How many baskets of fragments were taken up after the feeding of the five thousand?

    Twelve.   Mark 6:43

12. Did the disciples of Jesus always observe the Jewish customs?

    No.   Mark 7:2-3

13. Did Jesus consent to give the Pharisees a sign?

    No.   Mark 8:12

14. What answer did Peter give to the question by Jesus "Whom say ye that I am?

    "Thou art the Christ."   Mark 8:29

15. To which disciple did Jesus say, "Get thee behind me, Satan: for thou savourest not the things that be of God, but the things that be of men"?

    Peter.   Mark 8:33

16. When Jesus came down from the mount of transfiguration what did He find His disciples trying to do?

    To heal a man with a dumb spirit.   Mark 9:17

17. Was Jesus pleased when His disciples tried to keep Him from being bothered with those who brought young children to Him?

    No, He was displeased.   Mark 10:13-15

18. What did the other ten disciples think when two disciples asked to sit with Jesus in a place of honor?

    They were displeased.   Mark 10:41

19. What was happening when the people cried, "Hosanna; Blessed is He that cometh in the name of the Lord"?

    Jesus was entering Jerusalem in triumph.   Mark 11:9, 11

20. In the parable of the vineyard, what did the husbandman do after his servants and messengers had been killed? — He sent His only son. Mark 12:6

21. The Sadducees gave Jesus a trick question about a widow who was married to a number of brothers. How many brothers were there in this question? — Seven. Mark 12:20

22. Did the disciples of Jesus admire the Temple in Jerusalem? — Yes. Mark 13:1

23. Jesus said: "For the Son of man is as a man taking a far journey, who left his house, and . . ." What did He advise His disciples to do? — Watch. Mark 13:37

24. Did the disciples sent by Jesus prepare the upper room? — No, it was all prepared when they got there. Mark 14:16

25. What two things did Jesus do to the bread before He gave it to His disciples at the Last Supper in the upper room? — He blessed it and broke it. Mark 14:22

26. The disciples went out to what mountain after supper in the upper room? — The mount of Olives. Mark 14:26

27. Finish this sentence: "And He said, "Abba, Father, all things are possible unto Thee; take away this cup from me: nevertheless, not what I will, but _____." — "what thou wilt." Mark 14:36

28. When did a disciple of Jesus curse and swear? — Peter, when he denied Him. Mark 14:71

29. What did Bartimaeus do for a living? — He begged. Mark 10:46

30. Was anyone ever healed just by touching the garment of Jesus? — Yes. Mark 5:29

2-Base Questions

1. When Jesus healed the leper, did He tell him to go and tell anyone about it? — No. Mark 1:44

2. What two groups criticized Jesus for eating with publicans and sinners? — The scribes and Pharisees. Mark 2:16

3. What king ordered John the Baptist killed? — Herod. Mark 6:16

4. Who said, "I see men as trees, walking"? — The blind man whose sight Jesus restored. Mark 8:23-24

5. What did Peter want to do on the mount of transfiguration? — Make three tabernacles, or "tents." Mark 9:5

6. Finish this statement: "Suffer the little children to come _____." — "unto me, and forbid them not; for of such is the kingdom of God." Mark 10:14

7. When Jesus sent two disciples to bring a colt, what were they to say to anyone who questioned them? — "The Lord hath need of them." Mark 11:3

8. Finish this statement: "And thou shalt love the Lord thy God with all thy heart, and with all thy soul, and with all thy mind, and with all _____." — "thy strength." Mark 12:30

9. With what kind of ointment was Jesus anointed by a woman?

Spikenard.   Mark 14:3

10. Finish this verse: "So then, after the Lord had spoken unto them, He was received up into heaven, and sat ____."

"on the right hand of God."   Mark 16:19

3-Base Questions

1. Complete this statement: "I came not to call the righteous, but _____."

"sinners to repentance."   Mark 2:17

2. Finish this sentence: "And suddenly when they had looked round about, they saw no man any more, save ____."

"Jesus only with themselves."   Mark 9:8

3. Finish this sentence: "My house shall be called of all nations the _____."

"house of prayer."   Mark 11:17

4. What three disciples did Jesus take with Him when He went into the garden to pray?

Peter, James, John.   Mark 14:33

5. Supply the missing word: "But go your way, tell His disciples and _____."

"Peter."   Mark 16:7

Home-Run Questions

1. In what work was Levi the son of Alphaeus engaged when Jesus called him to follow Him?

Receiving custom, or "taxes."   Mark 2:14

2. Did Jesus say the Sabbath was made for man and not man for the Sabbath?

Yes.   Mark 2:27

3. Name ten of the twelve disciples.

Simon, James, John, Andrew, Philip, Bartholomew, Matthew, Thomas, James the son of Alphaeus, Thaddeus, Simon the Canaanite, and Judas.   Mark 3:16-19

4. How old was the daughter of Jairus?

Twelve years.   Mark 5:42

5. When Jesus fed the multitude from seven loaves, how many baskets of fragments were taken up?

Seven baskets.   Mark 8:8

6. What does *Boanerges* mean?

Sons of thunder.   Mark 3:17

7. Name the three disciples whom Jesus took with Him to the mount of transfiguration.

Peter, James, John.   Mark 9:2

8. What did the voice from the clouds say on the mount of transfiguration?

"This is my beloved Son; hear Him."   Mark 9:7

9. Who was the father of Bartimaeus?

Timaeus.   Mark 10:46

10. Did Jesus overthrow the tables and cages of those who sold doves?

No.   Mark 11:15

Sacrifice-Fly Questions

(If answered correctly, the runners advance. Batter is out.
Cannot be used with two out. Same rule applies to bunts.)

1. On what kind of a tree did Jesus wither the leaves? — Fig tree. — Mark 11:21
2. What kind of crown did the soldiers place on the head of Jesus? — A crown of thorns. — Mark 15:17
3. What did Joseph of Arimathea do? — He placed the body of Jesus in a sepulchre. — Mark 15:46

Bunt Questions

(Same rule as sacrifice.)

1. What was Jesus doing when He was in a ship and a storm came up? — Sleeping. — Mark 4:38
2. Which disciple denied Jesus? — Peter. — Mark 14:72

SET 5—TEAM "RED"

1-Base Questions

1.	Who created the heaven and the earth?	God.	Genesis 1:1
2.	Who killed Abel?	Cain.	Genesis 4:8
3.	When was the first rainbow?	After the Flood.	Genesis 9:13
4.	Who was the man who was willing to sacrifice his own son?	Abraham.	Genesis 22:10
5.	Who despised his birthright?	Esau.	Genesis 25:34
6.	Who dreamed that he saw a ladder reaching from earth to heaven?	Jacob.	Genesis 28:12
7.	Who had a coat of many colors?	Joseph.	Genesis 37:3
8.	What was the name of the brother of Moses who was to talk for him?	Aaron.	Exodus 4:14
9.	Who was hidden in a basket by a river and found by a princess?	Moses.	Exodus 2:2
10.	Around what city did the children of Israel march until the walls fell down?	Jericho.	Joshua 6:20
11.	Who lost his strength when his hair was cut?	Samson.	Judges 16:17
12.	Who fell off a seat backward and broke his neck?	Eli.	1 Samuel 4:18
13.	What was the name of the giant killed by David?	Goliath.	1 Samuel 17:23
14.	Who tried to kill David with a javelin?	Saul.	1 Samuel 18:11
15.	What queen came to ask Solomon questions?	Queen of Sheba.	1 Kings 10:1
16.	What queen went in before the king to save her people at the risk of her life?	Esther.	Esther 5:1
17.	Where in the Bible will you find the words "Blessed is the man that walketh not in the counsel of the ungodly"?	Psalm 1.	Psalm 1:1
18.	What book in the Bible comes after Isaiah?	Jeremiah.	
19.	Who was cast into the lions' den?	Daniel.	Daniel 6:16
20.	What king tried to find out where Jesus was born?	Herod.	Matthew 2:4
21.	Who baptized Jesus?	John.	Matthew 3:13
22.	To what city was Jesus taken on a visit when he was twelve years old?	Jerusalem.	Luke 2:42
23.	What guided the wise men to the place where Jesus was born?	A star.	Matthew 2:9
24.	Which of these were brothers? David and John, or Daniel and Peter, or Andrew and Simon?	Andrew and Simon.	John 1:40
25.	Who was converted while on the way to Damascus?	Paul.	Acts 26:13
26.	Whose father-in-law was Jethro of Midian?	Moses'.	Exodus 3:1
27.	What great teachings are found in the 5th chapter of Deuteronomy?	The Ten Commandments.	

28.	Whose mother-in-law was sick of a fever?	Simon Peter's.	Mark 1:30
29.	Finish this verse: "Blessed are the merciful _____."	"for they shall obtain mercy."	Matthew 5:7
30.	Finish this verse: "Blessed are the poor in spirit _____."	"for theirs is the kingdom of heaven."	Matthew 5:3

2-Base Questions

1.	Who said, "Am I my brother's keeper?"	Cain.	Genesis 4:9
2.	To whom did God say, "The place whereon thou standest is holy ground"?	Moses.	Exodus 3:5
3.	Who said, "Entreat me not to leave thee, or to return from following after thee: for whither thou goest, I will go; and where thou lodgest, I will lodge: thy people shall be my people, and thy God my God"?	Ruth.	Ruth 1:16
4.	Who said, "Thou comest to me with a sword, and with a spear, and with a shield: but I come to thee in the name of the Lord of hosts"?	David.	1 Samuel 17:45
5.	Who said, "Oh that one would give me to drink of the water of the well of Bethlehem"?	David.	1 Chronicles 11:17
6.	Who said, "Whose shoe's latchet I am not worthy to unloose"?	John the Baptist.	John 1:27
7.	Who said, "Take heed that ye do not your alms before men to be seen of them"?	Jesus.	Matthew 6:1
8.	Who said, "Let not your heart be troubled: ye believe in God, believe also in Me"?	Jesus.	John 14:1
9.	Who said, "Though I speak with the tongues of men and of angels, and have not charity, I am become as sounding brass, or a tinkling cymbal"?	Paul.	1 Corinthians 13:1
10.	Who said, "Lord, to whom should we go? Thou hast the words of eternal life"?	Peter.	John 6:68

3-Base Questions

1.	In whose house did Joseph serve as a slave?	Potiphar's.	Genesis 37:36
2.	Who made a vow that resulted in his killing his own daughter?	Jephthah.	Judges 11:34
3.	What was the name of the woman who betrayed Samson?	Delilah.	Judges 16:18
4.	Who was the mother of Samuel?	Hannah.	1 Samuel 2:21
5.	What king took Naboth's vineyard?	Ahab.	1 Kings 21:6

Home-Run Questions

1. Who was the lame young man to whom David showed kindness?	Mephibosheth.	2 Samuel 9:6
2. Who was the wife of King Ahab?	Jezebel.	1 Kings 21:5
3. How many wise men came from the East when Jesus was born?	The Bible does not say.	Matthew 2:1
4. Who was Isaac's wife?	Rebekah.	Genesis 24:67
5. Who was the father of Shem and Ham?	Noah.	Genesis 5:32
6. Who was the mother of John the Baptist?	Elizabeth.	Luke 1:13
7. The people were given a choice of having Jesus or what man released?	Barabbas.	Mark 15:7
8. Before what Roman ruler was Jesus tried?	Pilate.	Luke 23:1
9. Who was the husband of Drusilla?	Felix.	Acts 24:24
10. Who was the prophet who rebuked David for his sins?	Nathan.	2 Samuel 12:7

Sacrifice-Fly Questions

(If answered correctly, the runners advance. Batter is out. Cannot be used with two out. Same rule applies to bunts.)

1. Who betrayed Jesus with a kiss?	Judas.	Matthew 26:47-49
2. Whose head was cut off and brought in on a charger?	John the Baptist's.	Matthew 14:8, 11
3. What was Paul's name before he was converted?	Saul.	Acts 9:1

Bunt Questions

(Same rule as sacrifice.)

1. In what kind of bed was the baby Jesus laid?	A manger.	Luke 2:7
2. In what psalm do we find the words "The Lord is my shepherd: I shall not want"?	Psalm 23.	Psalm 23:1

SET 5—TEAM "BLUE"

1-Base Questions

1. In what garden did Adam and Eve live? — Eden. — Genesis 2:8
2. Who was the man who built an ark before a flood? — Noah. — Genesis 6:22
3. What was the name of the tower whose top was supposed to reach up to heaven? — Babel. — Genesis 11:9
4. What was the name of the wife who was found beside a well? — Rebekah. — Genesis 24:15
5. Whose wife was turned into a pillar of salt? — Lot's. — Genesis 19:26
6. Jacob served Laban for fourteen years to have what woman as his wife? — Rachel. — Genesis 29:28
7. Who turned aside to see a burning bush? — Moses. — Exodus 3:3
8. Who was ruler in Egypt when Moses brought out the children of Israel? — Pharaoh. — Exodus 14:5
9. Who became the leader of the children of Israel after Moses died? — Joshua. — Deuteronomy 34:9
10. Who led an army that was armed with lamps and pitchers? — Gideon. — Judges 7:19
11. Who thought he heard Eli the priest calling him when it was really God? — Samuel. — 1 Samuel 3:8
12. Was King Saul a tall man or a short man? — Tall. — 1 Samuel 9:2
13. Who was David's very close friend? — Jonathan. — 1 Samuel 20:17
14. Who became king after David? — Solomon. — 1 Kings 1:39
15. What prophet was fed by the ravens? — Elijah. — 1 Kings 17:6
16. What book in the Bible is about a man who was tempted by Satan with God's permission? — Job.
17. In what book in the Bible will you find the words "Remember now thy Creator in the days of thy youth"? — Ecclesiastes. — Ecclesiastes 12:1
18. What did the king do to Shadrach, Meshach, and Abednego? — Had them thrown into a fiery furnace. — Daniel 3:21
19. Where was Jesus born? — Bethlehem. — Matthew 2:1
20. To what country was Jesus taken when He was very young? — Egypt. — Matthew 2:14
21. Who was the brother of James the son of Zebedee? — John. — Matthew 4:21
22. In what city did Jesus spend His boyhood? — Nazareth. — Luke 2:39
23. Which of these two made a journey together? David and Lot, Solomon and Abraham, Paul and Barnabas? — Paul and Barnabas. — Acts 13:2
24. Which of these two were husband and wife? Timothy and Lydia, Jacob and Leah, David and Rachel. — Jacob and Leah. — Genesis 29:25

25.	In what book in the Bible will you find letters to seven churches?	Revelation.	Revelation 1:20
26.	What great teachings are found in the 20th chapter of Exodus?	The Ten Commandments.	
27.	In what book in the Bible do you find Naomi?	Ruth.	Ruth 1:2
28.	What did Jesus say a man should do before he cast the "mote" out of his brother's eye?	Cast the beam out of his own eye.	Matthew 7:5
29.	Finish this verse: "Blessed are the pure in heart _____."	"for they shall see God."	Matthew 5:8
30.	Finish this verse: "Blessed are they that mourn _____."	"for they shall be comforted."	Matthew 5:4

2-Base Questions

1.	Who said, "Surely the Lord is in this place and I knew it not"?	Jacob.	Genesis 28:16
2.	Who put forth the riddle "Out of the eater came forth meat, and out of the strong came forth sweetness"?	Samson.	Judges 14:14
3.	Who said, "Here am I," and, "Speak; for thy servant heareth"?	Samuel.	1 Samuel 3:4, 10
4.	Who said, "O Absalom, my son, my son"?	David.	2 Samuel 18:33
5.	Who said, "I am doing a great work, so that I cannot come down"?	Nehemiah.	Nehemiah 6:3
6.	In what book in the Bible will you find the words "Thou art weighed in the balances and art found wanting"?	Daniel.	Daniel 5:27
7.	Who said, "I can do all things through Christ which strengtheneth me"?	Paul.	Philippians 4:13
8.	To whom did Jesus say, "Today thou shalt be with me in paradise"?	The thief on the cross.	Luke 23:43
9.	Who said, "For my yoke is easy and my burden is light"?	Jesus.	Matthew 11:30
10.	Who said, "If God be for us, who can be against us"?	Paul.	Romans 8:31

3-Base Questions

1.	In whose sack of grain did a ruler have placed a silver cup?	Benjamin's.	Genesis 44:12
2.	What woman helped to lead an army?	Deborah.	Judges 4:10
3.	What was the word the Ephraimites were forced to use that betrayed their nationality?	Shibboleth.	Judges 12:6
4.	Who ate the shewbread?	David.	1 Samuel 21:6
5.	Of whose driving was it said "for he driveth furiously"?	Jehu.	2 Kings 9:20

Home-Run Questions

1. Who furnished Solomon with cedar trees?	Hiram.	1 Kings 5:10
2. Who was hung on his own gallows?	Haman.	Esther 7:10
3. Who was the father of Seth?	Adam.	Genesis 4:25
4. How old was Methuselah when he died?	969 years.	Genesis 5:27
5. Who ruled Rome when Jesus was born?	Caesar Augustus.	Luke 2:1
6. Who was the father of John the Baptist?	Zacharias.	Luke 1:13
7. Who went out from the trial of Jesus and wept bitterly?	Peter.	Matthew 26:75
8. In whose tomb was the body of Jesus buried?	Joseph of Arimathea's.	Matthew 27:59-60
9. Who was the wife of Uriah the Hittite?	Bathsheba.	2 Samuel 11:3
10. What was the sin of Ananias?	He lied.	Acts 5:3

Sacrifice-Fly Questions

(If answered correctly, the runners advance. Batter is out.
Cannot be used with two out. Same rule applies to bunts.)

1. Who came to Jesus by night?	Nicodemus.	John 3:1-2
2. Who named the birds and beasts?	Adam.	Genesis 2:20
3. Who was the mother of Jesus?	Mary.	Luke 2:7

Bunt Questions

(Same rule as sacrifice.)

1. Who "kept all these things and pondered them in her heart"?	Mary.	Luke 2:19
2. What was the work of Simon Peter before he left it to follow Jesus?	He was a fisherman.	Matthew 4:18

SET 6—TEAM "RED"
1-Base Questions

1. How long was Jesus on earth after He rose from the dead? — Forty days. Acts 1:3
2. Who said, "Ye men of Galilee, why stand ye gazing up to heaven?" — Two men in white apparel. Acts 1:10
3. When the day of Pentecost was fully come, what were the disciples doing? — They were all with one accord in one place. Acts 2:1
4. What were the cloven tongues at Pentecost like? — Fire. Acts 2:3
5. Why was the multitude confounded at Pentecost? — Because they heard every man in his own language. Acts 2:6
6. Who answered those who mocked the disciples at Pentecost? — Peter. Acts 2:14
7. What did the early followers of Jesus do with their possessions? — Sold them. Acts 2:45
8. At what Temple gate did a lame man beg from Peter and John? — Beautiful. Acts 3:2
9. Who was the Prince of Life? — Jesus. Acts 3:15
10. What did Ananias and Sapphira do? — Lied to the Holy Ghost, holding out part of their possessions. Acts 5:1-2
11. Who said to the disciples, "Go, stand and speak in the temple to the people all the words of this life"? — The angel of the Lord. Acts 5:19-20
12. How did the apostles solve the problem caused by the dispute about the distribution of food? — They appointed men to take care of it. Acts 6:5
13. Who was the first martyr? — Stephen. Acts 7:60
14. Who stood consenting to the death of Stephen? — Saul. Acts 8:1
15. What did the members of the early church who were scattered abroad do? — Preached. Acts 8:4
16. Who tried to purchase the gift of the Holy Ghost with money? — Simon the sorcerer. Acts 8:19
17. Why had the Ethiopian whom Philip met been in Jerusalem? — To worship. Acts 8:27
18. To what city did Saul ask letters to continue his persecution of the church? — Damascus. Acts 9:2
19. Who appeared to Saul on the road to Damascus? — Jesus. Acts 9:5
20. How long did Saul go without food and water after the vision on the road to Damascus? — Three days. Acts 9:9
21. To what people was Saul to bear the name of the Lord? — The Gentiles. Acts 9:15
22. Who baptized Saul? — Ananias. Acts 9:17
23. How did the disciples get Saul out of Damascus? — They let him down over the wall in a basket. Acts 9:25
24. What did the "Greeks" in Jerusalem want to do with Saul? — Kill him. Acts 9:29
25. Who went to visit the saints at Lydda? — Peter. Acts 9:32

26.	What was the characteristic of Dorcas?	She was full of good works.	Acts 9:36
27.	What was the first thing Peter did when he came into the room where they had the body of Dorcas?	Put everyone out.	Acts 9:40
28.	Who was the father of Isaac?	Abraham.	Acts 7:8
29.	Who did God deliver from his afflictions and make governor of Egypt?	Joseph.	Acts 7:10
30.	What animal did the children of Israel make as an idol?	A calf.	Acts 7:41

2-Base Questions

1.	When Jesus ascended to heaven, what took Him out of the sight of the disciples?	A cloud.	Acts 1:9
2.	Who was selected as apostle by prayer and the drawing of lots?	Matthias.	Acts 1:26
3.	Who said, "This is the stone which was set at nought of you builders, which is become the head of the corner"?	Peter.	Acts 4:8, 11
4.	Finish this verse: "It is not reason that we should _____."	"leave the word of God, and serve tables."	Acts 6:2
5.	Finish this verse: "And Philip opened his mouth, and began at the same scripture _____."	"and preached unto him Jesus."	Acts 8:35
6.	Finish this verse: "For I will show him how great things he must _____."	"suffer for my name's sake."	Acts 9:16
7.	In what city did Dorcas live?	Joppa.	Acts 9:36
8.	In the wilderness of what mountain did the Lord appear to Moses in a burning bush?	Sinai.	Acts 7:30
9.	Finish this verse: "Behold, I see the heavens opened, and the Son of man _____."	"standing on the right hand of God."	Acts 7:56
10.	Finish this verse: "Till another king arose, which knew not _____."	"Joseph."	Acts 7:18

3-Base Questions

1.	Did Ananias and Sapphira stand up together and talk to Peter?	No.	Acts 5:7
2.	In what country did Philip first preach?	Samaria.	Acts 8:5
3.	In what street was the house where Saul went after his vision?	The street called Straight.	Acts 9:11
4.	Where did Saul go after he left Damascus?	To Jerusalem.	Acts 9:26
5.	Where did the brethren send Saul from Jerusalem?	To Caesarea and Tarsus.	Acts 9:30

Home-Run Questions

1. How many people assembled in an upper room after the ascension of Jesus?

   One hundred twenty.   Acts 1:15

2. Who was Joseph called Barsabas?

   One of the two considered to take the place of Judas.   Acts 1:23

3. What great king of Israel was quoted at Pentecost?

   David.   Acts 2:25

4. At what hour did Peter and John go up to the Temple to pray?

   Ninth hour.   Acts 3:1

5. Of what sect was the high priest?

   The Sadducees.   Acts 5:17

6. What did the apostles do before they chose someone to take the place of Judas and before they ordained helpers?

   Prayed.   Acts 1:24   Acts 6:4

7. Who was Timon?

   One of the men selected to administer food.   Acts 6:5

8. When the persecution first started, where did the apostles go?

   They didn't go—they stayed in Jerusalem.   Acts 8:1

9. In what direction did a man travel to go from Jerusalem to Gaza?

   South.   Acts 8:26

10. How long had Aeneas been sick in bed?

    Eight years.   Acts 9:33

Sacrifice-Fly Questions

(If answered correctly, the runners advance. Batter is out. Cannot be used with two out. Same rule applies to bunts.)

1. With what did John baptize?

   Water.   Acts 1:5

2. What did Peter do for the lame man at the gate of the Temple?

   Healed him.   Acts 3:8

3. Were Peter and John well-educated men?

   No.   Acts 4:13

Bunt Questions

(Same rule as sacrifice.)

1. Was Gaza a place of fertile lands?

   No.   Acts 8:26

2. Who is described as breathing out threatenings and slaughter against the disciples of the Lord?

   Saul.   Acts 9:1

SET 6 — TEAM "BLUE"

1-Base Questions

1. Were the disciples to witness unto Jesus just in Palestine? — No. Acts 1:8
2. Who spoke to the disciples about Judas the traitor? — Peter. Acts 1:15-16
3. What was the sound at Pentecost like? — A rushing mighty wind. Acts 2:2
4. With what were the disciples filled at Pentecost? — The Holy Ghost. Acts 2:4
5. What did the mocking people say about the disciples at Pentecost? — They said they were intoxicated (full of new wine). Acts 2:13
6. What did Peter say his listeners at Pentecost should do? — Repent and be baptized. Acts 2:38
7. What group of people had all things in common and did eat their meat with gladness and singleness of heart? — The early followers of Jesus. Acts 2:46
8. Who said, "Silver and gold have I none, but such as I have give I thee"? — Peter. Acts 3:6
9. What did Peter and John say when the ruler told them to quit preaching? — They refused to quit. Acts 4:20
10. What happened to Ananias and Sapphira? — They were struck dead. Acts 5:5, 10
11. Why did the Grecians in the company of Christians murmur against the Hebrews? — They said their widows were neglected in the daily ministration. Acts 6:1
12. How did the apostles ordain the men who were to be their special helpers? — They laid their hands on them. Acts 6:6
13. What kind of men carried Stephen to his burial? — Devout men. Acts 8:2
14. What charge was made against Stephen? — That he blasphemed. Acts 6:13
15. Did the people to whom Philip first preached believe? — Yes. Acts 8:12
16. Who told Philip to travel to another place to preach? — The angel of the Lord. Acts 8:26
17. What did Philip say the Ethiopian must do in order to be baptized? — Believe with all his heart. Acts 8:37
18. Did Saul seek to bring just the men disciples bound unto Jerusalem? — No, he included the women. Acts 9:2
19. What was the physical affliction of Saul after the vision on the road to Damascus? — He was blind. Acts 9:9
20. When the Lord told Ananias to go to Saul, had Ananias ever heard of Saul before? — Yes. Acts 9:13
21. How did Ananias first address Saul? — Brother Saul. Acts 9:17
22. Did Saul eat right after he was baptized? — Yes. Acts 9:19
23. What did the disciples think when Saul tried to join them in Jerusalem? — They were afraid of him. Acts 9:26

24.	After the conversion of Saul, did the church enjoy any rest from persecution?	Yes.	Acts 9:31
25.	What disease did Aeneas have?	Palsy.	Acts 9:33
26.	Was Lydda far from Joppa?	No.	Acts 9:38
27.	What was the business of Simon of Joppa?	He was a tanner.	Acts 9:43
28.	Who was the father of Jacob?	Isaac.	Acts 7:8
29.	Why did Jacob send men down into Egypt?	To get corn.	Acts 7:12
30.	Who took Moses and reared him as her own son?	Pharaoh's daughter.	Acts 7:21

2-Base Questions

1.	From what mountain did Jesus ascend to heaven?	Olivet.	Acts 1:12
2.	Of what language group were the disciples?	Galilean.	Acts 2:7
3.	Finish this verse: "We ought to obey _____."	"God rather than men."	Acts 5:29
4.	When the people of Samaria accepted the Word of God what two men did the apostles send to them?	Peter and John.	Acts 8:14
5.	Finish this verse: "And he fell to the earth, and heard a voice saying unto him, Saul, Saul, _____."	"why persecutest thou me?"	Acts 9:4
6.	Which one of the apostles brought healing to Aeneas?	Peter.	Acts 9:34
7.	How old was Moses when he killed the Egyptian?	Forty years old.	Acts 7:23-24
8.	Who said, "The most high dwelleth not in temples made with hands"?	Stephen.	Acts 7:48
9.	Who said, "Which of the prophets have not your fathers persecuted? and they have slain them which showed before of the coming of the Just One, of whom ye have been now the betrayers and murderers"?	Stephen.	Acts 7:52
10.	What did Abraham buy from the sons of Emmor?	A sepulchre.	Acts 7:16

3-Base Questions

1.	To whose speech is nearly all of the seventh chapter of Acts given?	Stephen's.	Acts 7
2.	From what prophet was the Ethiopian reading when Philip saw him?	Esaias.	Acts 8:28
3.	Did Ananias of Damascus go to Saul and also lie about his possessions?	No. They were two different men.	Acts 5:1

4. In whose house was Ananias to meet Saul? Judas's. Acts 9:11
5. Give another name for Dorcas. Tabitha. Acts 9:36

Home-Run Questions

1. What does Aceldama mean? The field of blood. Acts 1:19
2. What prophet did Peter quote in his defense of the disciples at Pentecost? Joel. Acts 2:16
3. How many people were converted at Pentecost? About 3,000. Acts 2:41
4. What does Barnabas mean? The son of consolation. Acts 4:36
5. Who said, "For if this counsel or this work be of men, it will come to naught: But if it be of God, ye cannot overthrow it"? Gamaliel. Acts 5:34, 38-39
6. Of what sect was Gamaliel? A Pharisee. Acts 5:34
7. When the persecution started, to what two regions did the followers of Jesus go? Judea and Samaria. Acts 8:1
8. Who was the man using sorcery whom Philip encountered? Simon. Acts 8:9
9. Under what queen did the Ethiopian Philip met serve? Candace. Acts 8:27
10. Where did Abraham live before he lived in Charran? Mesopotamia. Acts 7:2

Sacrifice-Fly Questions

(If answered correctly, the runners advance. Batter is out. Cannot be used with two out. Same rule applies to bunts.)

1. Was anyone chosen to take the place of Judas? Yes. Acts 1:26
2. In what building was Solomon's porch? The Temple. Acts 3:11
3. Who made havoc of the early church? Saul. Acts 8:3

Bunt Questions

(Same rule as sacrifice.)

1. In what was the Ethiopian riding when Philip saw him? A chariot. Acts 8:28
2. Did Paul preach in Damascus? Yes. Acts 9:20

SET 7—TEAM "RED"

1-Base Questions

1. What time did Cornelius see a vision? — The ninth hour. — Acts 10:3
2. At whose house was Peter when Cornelius had his vision? — Simon the tanner's. — Acts 10:6
3. How many men did Cornelius send to Peter? — Three. — Acts 10:7
4. Why would Peter in his trance not kill and eat the animals he saw? — He had never eaten anything considered common or unclean. — Acts 10:14
5. How many times did the vision of Peter's about the many animals occur? — Three times. — Acts 10:16
6. Did Peter go right away when the men came? — No, "on the morrow." — Acts 10:23
7. What did Peter say was unlawful for a Jew? — To keep company or come unto one of another nation. — Acts 10:28
8. What happened to those who heard Peter at the home of Cornelius? — The Holy Ghost fell on them. — Acts 10:44
9. What did Peter do to those Gentiles on whom the Holy Ghost came? — Commanded that they should be baptized. — Acts 10:48
10. What did Peter do when criticized for eating with Gentiles? — Peter rehearsed the matter from the beginning. — Acts 11:4
11. What was the conclusion of those who heard Peter tell how the Holy Ghost fell on the Gentiles too? — They held their peace and glorified God, saying, Then hath God also to the Gentiles granted repentance unto life. — Acts 11:18
12. What reason can you give that would show those who spoke to the Greeks also were doing the right thing? — "And the hand of the Lord was with them: and a great number believed, and turned unto the Lord." — Acts 11:21
13. Did Saul come when Barnabas sought him in Tarsus? — Yes. — Acts 11:26
14. What did Agabus, one of the prophets who came from Jerusalem to Antioch, warn about? — "And there stood up Agabus, and signified by the Spirit that there should be great dearth throughout all the world." — Acts 11:28
15. What did Herod stretch forth? Why? — "Herod the king stretched forth his hands to vex certain of the church." — Acts 12:1
16. Was Peter awake when the angel came? — No. — Acts 12:6
17. What reason can you give to show that Peter did not expect this visitation of the angel when he was in prison? — He was not dressed. — Acts 12:8
18. How far did the angel accompany Peter as he was freed from prison? — Out of the prison and on through one street. — Acts 12:10
19. What were the people doing when Peter arrived at the home of Mary, mother of John? — Praying. — Acts 12:12
20. How did Saul and Barnabas get to Cyprus? — Sailed. — Acts 13:4

51

21. What did the Gentiles ask of Paul in Antioch of Pisidia after he had preached in the synagogue?

"The Gentiles besought that these words might be preached to them the next Sabbath." Acts 13:42

22. What names were given to Paul and Barnabas when they were in Lystra?

"And they called Barnabas, Jupiter; and Paul, Mercurius." Acts 14:12

23. When Paul was stoned, dragged outside a city, and left for dead, what happened?

"Howbeit as the disciples stood around about him, he rose up, and came into the city." Acts 14:20

24. Finish the sentence: "And being brought on their way by the church, they passed through Phenice and Samaria, declaring the conversion of the Gentiles: and they caused _____."

"great joy unto all the brethren." Acts 15:3

25. Who among the apostles and elders first gave answer to the controversy among the Christians about keeping the laws of Moses?

Peter. Acts 15:7

26. Who was the second among the apostles and elders to give answer to the controversy among the Christians over the laws of Moses?

James. Acts 15:13

27. Whom did Paul choose from Derbe and Lystra to accompany him?

Timothy. Acts 16:3

28. What was the name of the lady who was a seller of purple?

Lydia. Acts 16:14

29. When Paul was in Athens, to what hill did the Athenians bring him to hear him speak?

Mars Hill. Acts 17:22

30. Complete the sentence, "And when they opposed themselves, and blasphemed, he shook his raiment, and said unto them, Your blood be upon your own heads; I am clean: from henceforth _____."

"I will go unto the Gentiles." Acts 18:6

2-Base Questions

1. What did Peter say when Cornelius worshiped him?

"Stand up; I myself also am a man." Acts 10:26

2. What kind of reception did Peter receive when he arrived in Jerusalem?

They contended with him. Acts 11:2

3. What did they say to Peter about his visit to Cornelius?

"Thou wentest in unto men uncircumcized, and didst eat with them." Acts 11:3

4. What did Peter say happened when he began to speak to the Gentiles at Cornelius's home?

"The Holy Ghost fell on them, as on us at the beginning." Acts 11:15

5. Repeat the angel's words and tell what occurred to Peter's chains.

"Arise up quickly. And his chains fell off from his hands." Acts 12:7

6. Who was the first martyred of the apostles and how was he killed?

James the brother of John, by the sword. Acts 12:2

7. What proof is there that Paul's prophecy about Elymas the sorcerer came true?

"And immediately there fell on him a mist and a darkness, and he went about seeking some to lead him by the hand." Acts 13:11

8. Why didn't Paul and his party go into Asia to preach?

"And were forbidden of the Holy Ghost to preach the word in Asia." Acts 16:6

9. In Lystra, Paul healed a man crippled in his feet—what did the people assert about Paul and Barnabas?

"The gods are come down to us in the likeness of men." Acts 14:11

10. Complete the sentence: "And when they had preached the gospel to that city, and had taught many, they returned again to Lystra, and to Iconium, and Antioch, confirming the souls of the disciples and exhorting them to continue in the faith, and that we must through _____."

"much tribulation enter into the kingdom of God." Acts 14:22

3-Base Questions

1. What did Peter say the attitude of the Spirit was in reference to Jew and Gentile?

The Spirit bade him go with them, nothing doubting." Acts 11:12

2. What was Agabus?

A prophet. Acts 11:27-28

3. At what time did the martyrdom of James take place?

The days of unleavened bread. Acts 12:3

4. Complete the sentence "Now I know of a surety, that the Lord hath sent his angel, and hath delivered _____."

"me out of the hand of Herod, and from all the expectation of the people of the Jews." Acts 12:11

5. What was the answer of Paul and Silas to the jailer when he asked Paul, "Sirs, what must I do to be saved?"

"Believe on the Lord Jesus Christ, and thou shalt be saved, and thy house." Acts 16:31

Home-Run Questions

1. What were the words of John the Baptist that Peter quoted?

"John indeed baptized with water; but ye shall be baptized with the Holy Ghost." Acts 11:16

2. What kind of a man was Barnabas?

"He was a good man, and full of the Holy Ghost and of faith." Acts 11:24

3. Give the words that show that the famine prophesied by Agabus came.

". . . which came to pass in the days of Claudius Caesar." Acts 11:28

4. How many soldiers were to watch over Peter in prison?

Four quaternions. Acts 12:4

5. Why didn't the girl open the gate to Peter when he came from prison?

"She opened not the gate for gladness." Acts 12:14

6. Finish the verse, "O full of all subtilty and all mischief, thou child of the devil, thou enemy of all righteousness, wilt thou not _____."

"cease to pervert the right ways of the Lord?" Acts 13:10

7. Complete the sentence, "Men and brethren, ye know how that a good while ago God made choice among us, that the Gentiles by my _____."

"mouth should hear the word of the gospel, and believe." Acts 15:7

8. By what words did James show that he was head of the Jerusalem church?

"Wherefore my sentence is . . ." Acts 15:19

9. Complete the sentence, "For he mightily convinced the Jews, and that publicly, showing by the scriptures that _____."

Jesus was Christ." Acts 18:28

10. Finish the sentence, "And Paul, as his manner was, went in unto them, and three sabbath days reasoned with them out of the scriptures, opening and alleging that _____."

"Christ must needs have suffered, and risen again from the dead; and that this Jesus, whom I preach unto you, is Christ." Acts 17:3

Sacrifice-Fly Questions

(If answered correctly, the runners advance. Batter is out. Cannot be used with two out. Same rule applies to bunts.)

1. How was social service applied toward the brethren in Judea?

The disciples sent relief, according to their ability. Acts 11:29-30

2. Fill in the missing words, "And when they had _____ them elders in every church, and had _____ with _____, they commended them to the Lord, on whom they _____."

ordained, prayed, fasting, believed. Acts 14:23

3. Complete the sentence, "These that have turned the world _____."

"upside down are come hither also." Acts 17:6

Bunt Questions

(Same rule as sacrifice.)

1. Whom did Barnabas and Saul take with them when they went back to Antioch?

John, surnamed Mark. Acts 12:25

2. Give two items included in the report of Paul and Barnabas to the church of Antioch in Syria after the first missionary journey.

"And when they were come, . . . they rehearsed all that God had done with them, and how He had opened the door of faith unto the Gentiles." Acts 14:27

SET 7 – TEAM "BLUE"

1-Base Questions

1. Where did Cornelius live? — Caesarea. — Acts 10:1
2. What was the location of Simon the tanner's house? — By the seaside. — Acts 10:6
3. Why did Peter go to the housetop? — To pray. — Acts 10:9
4. What time did Peter go up on the housetop of Simon the tanner's house? — Sixth hour. — Acts 10:9
5. Did Cornelius and Peter have their visions on the same day? — No. — Acts 10:9
6. Did Peter understand the vision of the vessel of all manner of animals when he saw it? — He doubted what it meant. — Acts 10:17
7. Was it a private meeting between Cornelius and Peter? If not, who was there? — No. Cornelius's kinsmen and friends. — Acts 10:24
8. What did Peter learn from the vision he had? — Not to call any man common or unclean. — Acts 10:28
9. Why were the Jews with Peter astonished? — Because the Holy Ghost was poured out on the Gentiles. — Acts 10:45
10. Who in Judea heard that the Gentiles had received the Word of God? — The apostles and brethren. — Acts 11:1
11. When Peter saw that the Gentiles received the Holy Ghost, what was his conclusion of the matter? — "What was I, that I could withstand God?" — Acts 11:17
12. How far did the Christians travel when Stephen was stoned? — As far as Phenice, and Cyprus, and Antioch. — Acts 11:19
13. What did Barnabas do when he came to the people of the dispersion at Antioch? — He exhorted them to cleave unto the Lord. — Acts 11:23
14. How long did Saul and Barnabas stay at Antioch? — A year. — Acts 11:26
15. Who took the gifts to the sufferers in Jerusalem? — Barnabas and Saul. — Acts 11:30
16. Herod intended to bring Peter out after what occasion? — Easter. — Acts 12:4
17. How did the angel awaken Peter? — He smote Peter on the side and raised him up, saying, "Arise up quickly." — Acts 12:7
18. What Scripture can you give to show that Peter didn't believe what was happening to him when he was led out of prison? — "And he went out, and followed him; and wist not that it was true which was done by the angel; but thought he saw a vision." — Acts 12:9
19. Where did Peter go when he was released from prison? — The house of Mary the mother of John. — Acts 12:12
20. What did Peter do while the girl was talking with the people, leaving him standing at the door of Mary's house? — Peter continued knocking. — Acts 12:16

21. Fill in the words: "As they ministered to the Lord, and fasted, the Holy Ghost said, Separate me _____ and _____ for the work whereunto I have called them."

Barnabas and Saul. Acts 13:2

22. Did Sergius Paulus believe Paul's teachings were right? Quote the verse.

"Then the deputy, when he saw what was done, believed, being astonished at the doctrine of the Lord." Acts 13:12

23. What did Paul and Barnabas do when the people with the priest of Jupiter would make sacrifice to them?

They rent their clothes. Acts 14:14

24. What did the Jews teach the people of Antioch that caused Paul and Barnabas to go to Jerusalem about it?

"Except ye be circumcised after the manner of Moses, ye cannot be saved." Acts 15:1

25. Of what sect were the men who believed but declared it was necessary for Christians to keep all of the law of Moses?

Pharisees. Acts 15:5

26. What difference did the Holy Ghost put between the Gentile Christians and the Jewish Christians?

"And put no difference between us and them, purifying their hearts by faith." Acts 15:9

27. Whom did Paul choose to take with him on his second missionary journey?

Silas. Acts 15:40

28. Describe Paul's vision in Troas.

"There stood a man of Macedonia, and prayed him, saying, Come over into Macedonia, and help us." Acts 16:9

29. How many of the household of the jailer—where Paul and Silas sang until an earthquake opened the doors of the jail—were baptized?

"He and all his." Acts 16:33

30. What did Paul find as an inscription on an altar in Athens?

"To the unknown God." Acts 17:23

2-Base Questions

1. Finish the sentence, "What God hath cleansed, _____."

"that call not thou common." Acts 10:15

2. Name two things Peter said was God's attitude toward men.

No respecter of persons; he that feareth him and worketh righteousness is accepted. Acts 10:34-35

3. When Peter returned to Jerusalem from Cornelius's home, who contended with him?

They that were of the circumcision. Acts 11:2

4. What did Peter say the Holy Spirit had told the centurion would be the content of the words of Peter?

"Words whereby thou and all thy house shall be saved." Acts 11:14

5. Finish the phrase "preaching the word to none but _____."

unto the Jews only. Acts 11:19

6. What did the people answer the girl who told them Peter was out of prison and at the gate?

"Thou art mad." Acts 12:15

7. What three things did the prophets and teachers at Antioch do for Barnabas and Saul before they sent them away?

Fasted, prayed, laid hands on them.
Acts 13:3

8. What filled the hearts of the Jews when they saw the multitudes that came to hear Paul when he preached to the Gentiles in Antioch of Pisidia?

Envy.
Acts 13:45

9. Complete the sentence "And these all do contrary to the decrees of Caesar, saying _____."

"that there is another king, one Jesus."
Acts 17:7

10. What was the difference between the Jews at Thessalonica and those of Berea?

"These were more noble than those in Thessalonica."
Acts 17:11

3-Base Questions

1. Name five things describing Cornelius.

Centurion, devout, feared God, gave alms, prayed.
Acts 10:1-2

2. Finish the sentence "But there were some of them men of Cyprus and Cyrene, who, when they were come to Antioch, spake _____."

"unto the Grecians, preaching the Lord Jesus."
Acts 11:20

3. What was the reaction of the Jews when they persecuted the church?

They were pleased.
Acts 12:3

4. How securely bound was Peter when Herod had him in prison?

He was bound with two chains, and keepers were before the door.
Acts 12:6

5. Complete the verse "And now, behold, the hand of the Lord is upon thee, and thou _____."

"shalt be blind."
Acts 13:11

Home-Run Questions

1. Describe Peter's answer to the Jews who objected that Peter ate with Gentiles.

Acts 11:5-11

2. What did the church at Jerusalem do about the people of the Dispersion when news of them came?

They sent forth Barnabas, who was to go as far as Antioch.
Acts 11:22

3. What significant name was given for the first time to the followers of Jesus at Antioch?

Christian.
Acts 11:26

4. The reaction of the Jews toward the persecution of the church caused Herod to do another act. What was it?

He put Peter in prison.
Acts 12:3-4

5. When Peter was in prison what did the church people do? Can you give the words describing their fervency?

"Prayer was made without ceasing of the church unto God for him."
Acts 12:5

6. Acts 13:9 gives a change in the way a certain missionary was addressed from that time on. What was it?

"Saul (who also is called Paul)."
Acts 13:9

7. Finish the sentence "Of this man's seed hath God according to His promise raised _____." | "unto Israel a Saviour, Jesus."
Acts 13:23

8. Peter asked a question. Fill in the words: "Now therefore why _____ ye God, to put a _____ upon the _____ of the disciples, which neither our _____ nor _____ were able to bear?" | tempt, yoke, neck, fathers, we
Acts 15:10

9. What four things were to be required of the Gentiles instead of all of the ceremonial laws of Moses, as settled upon by the council at Jerusalem? | "That they abstain from pollutions of idols, and from fornication, and from things strangled, and from blood."
Acts 15:20

10. Fill in the missing words: "But the Jews which believed not, moved with _____, took unto them certain _____ fellows of the _____ sort, and gathered a _____, and set all the city on an _____, and assaulted the house of _____, and sought to bring them out to the people." | envy, lewd, baser, company, uproar, Jason.
Acts 17:5

Sacrifice-Fly Questions

(If answered correctly, the runners advance. Batter is out. Cannot be used with two out. Same rule applies to bunts.)

1. Where did Barnabas go to seek a helper? | Tarsus. | Acts 11:25
2. What was the girl's name who came to the door of the gate of Mary the mother of John? | Rhoda. | Acts 12:13
3. What was the name of the sorcerer at Paphos? | Bar-jesus. | Acts 13:6

Bunt Questions

(Same rule as sacrifice.)

1. What caused the Dispersion? | The persecution about Stephen.
Acts 11:19
2. Who opened the gate of the prison when the angel freed Peter? | It opened of its own accord. | Acts 12:10

Score Cards for Games

Score Cards for Games

Score Cards for Games

Score Cards for Games